Lorne
FOREWORD

SHOTS

YOUTH ATHLETE RECRUITMENT GUIDE
the athlete edition

Shots Up! Youth Athlete Recruitment Guide: The Athlete Edition

Copyright © 2020 by Lorne Bowman, Sr.
Book Cover Design: ADEI Media Group

ADEI Media Group
Southfield, MI 48075
800.507.5090
contact@adeimedia.com
adeimedia.com

ISBN-13: 978-1-7358084-1-3

Printed in the United States of America. All rights reserved under International Copyright Law. Contents and/or cover may not be reproduced in whole or part in any form without the express written consent of the author, Lorne Bowman, Sr.

DEDICATION

First, I want to thank my Lord and Savior, Jesus Christ for giving me the inspiration to put my experiences into words. I would like to dedicate this book to my three beautiful children, Mariah, Lorne Jr., and Aaron who are my reasons why I get up to take it to the max every day. Also, I'd like to dedicate this book to the entire Bowman family whom I love very much. To my Dad and Mom, Bishop Andrew, and Viveca Merritt, and the entire Merritt family.

To every coach and trainer that took the time to sow your gifts and talents into my son over the years. To all my basketball brotherhood of friends who been so supportive throughout this journey; and to all my friends and well-wishers.

May God bless you all.

Lorne Bowman, Sr.

FOREWORD

Basketball has been a major part of my life since I was around 3 years old. I love the game and have enjoyed it for as long as I can remember. It has taught me so much and allowed me to grow into the person I am today. I gradually got better year after year until the point where college coaches started to take notice.

For myself and my family the recruitment process happened all of a sudden, and it happened fast. I was the first person in my family to go through a recruitment process so everything we did, we had to learn on our own. There wasn't anyone to guide us and teach things to watch out for or help us go through the process smoother.

Shots Up! provides a major tool that gives, both athletes and parents, more tips and guidelines that can make the recruitment process transition a lot easier. It would have been a huge benefit to me and my family, if more information had been provided about the recruitment process in the beginning.

To your success,

Cassius Winston

Big Ten Player of the Year (2019)
2x First team All-Big Ten (2018) (2019)
Big Ten Tournament: Most Outstanding Player (2019)
Michigan Mr. Basketball (2016)
Jordan Brand Classic All Star (2016)

INTRODUCING SHOTS UP!

Before you go any further down this path of athletics you will need to answer the most pressing question of all. Do you want to continue to play sports? I know it might seem like a bad time to ask you this, especially if you have been playing for a while. But the sooner you are honest with yourself and those around you about the intensity of your interest, the quicker you can start resolving any conflicts over the decision to take the recruiting journey seriously.

As I write this book, my son, Lorne Jr. will be leaving home to further his journey at the University of Wisconsin Madison, but he too had a period when he wasn't sure if he really wanted to go all the way in this process. So, I had to ask him the same question. As hard as it was for me to do, I waited on his answer.

When he did come around to the decision to continue to play the sport that he loved, I was there to support him. For some of you the answer may be that you don't want to continue, but your parents, friends, or other family may see that you have a gift and want you to use it. They may continue to push you in that direction.

You might be asking, "How do I handle this?" The best advice I can give you is to sit down with your parent and have a conversation. If you guys don't have an understanding, then you only have one other option; continue to play and give your best while you continue to have conversations about what you would like to do instead of sports.

Honoring your parents will have even greater rewards in your life and things will turn around for you as you keep the right attitude and think of this as an opportunity to give your best. Plus, as we move forward in this book, we will talk about how sports can turn into an advantage for you doing the things that you love in the future outside of athletics.

Ultimately, this book is to get you to think about your future and going to the next level in life, no matter which path you choose to take.

CAPTURE THE QUEST

Take a moment to answer this question: Do you want to play sports? Why? Or Why not?

_____
_____
_____
_____
_____
_____

SEASONS

Life is about seasons. The older I get, the more I understand this fundamental truth and you will too. We have some areas of life where seasons come around again and again. Yet there are others that don't come around as often, if ever in a lifetime. However, what I do know is that every season has a purpose. Believe me when I tell you that this season of your life not only holds great potential, but great opportunity as well. I want to be one of the people that help you uncover all that this season of your life has to offer in terms of athletics and college recruitment.

I made Shots Up! easy to navigate by dividing it up into three sections.

Pre-Season or Training Camp

In this section, we will discuss what happens before the recruiting phase starts. We will talk about a few things like:

- Cultivating mindset and building character.
- Building consistency in your game play.
- How to handle failures with dignity.

All these critical elements have either been witnessed or experienced during my journey with athletes and can help, hinder, or blindside your chances for advancement in the recruitment stage. Training camp or pre-season as it is, offers a time to build up areas of weakness and should not be overlooked or taken for granted.

Recruitment or Regular Season

Make no mistake. Recruitment is a season!

There is so much preparation, politics, and process that goes into the behind-the-scenes of not only getting you ready for next level play, if that is the path that they are going to take; but of other considerations that may have never crossed your mind. Even the small things that seem innocent on the outside can be dangerous for your career if you don't know how to navigate the things well.

Getting through recruitment is going to be intense and require discipline more than any of the other two seasons. Unlike training camp, everything counts in this season and for some, it can be a stressful and completely overwhelming time. Just remember, Shots Up! was written to help you through it. Know that you are not alone.

Post-Season or 'Select and Sign'

You made it to the post-season! Now we get to talk about reaping some of the rewards and reviewing the playbook that we used to get to this point.

You and your family have left it all on the court; but you can't celebrate too hard or too long at this stage. There are some additional key takeaways that can position you for a college career that launches your success for years to come. That's what this is all about, right?

I want you to experience success on every level and in every season of life. That's where my heart and desire come from in writing this book. Yes, Shots Up! is about recruitment, but it's also about even more than that. It's about relationships. The relationship you have with your family and the game, with its process, and the potential rewards that are waiting for you once the process is over. This will ultimately go beyond the game play and help create a mindset that builds character, perseverance, and more relationships with others throughout your lifetime— no matter where you find yourself, on or off the court.

CAPTURE THE QUEST

Answer the questions below.

What are you looking to get out of Shots Up!

_____
_____
_____
_____
_____
_____

Which season are you in?

_____
_____
_____

SECTION ONE
PRE-SEASON PREPARATION

"My son shot the ball and kept his hand extended with great form after that release." (Hmm)

I had taken him to Dave and Busters, where he played the 'pop-a-shot machine' where you shoot the basketball in the net to land a prize. It was my first mental note of his potential.

He was 2.

As he got older, I noticed that he had a genuine interest in the game, which over time continued to increase. Then came bigger and taller rims with near perfect form, extension, and follow-through.

He was only 4 or 5 by then.

By the time my son was six years old, I had already taken the initiative to see if this was something that he might really want to take more seriously.

Turns out, he did. And for many of you, you have too. So, let's discuss what it takes to be more than the talent you have and the skillset you possess. Let's talk about the things that don't show up on the scoreboard in the stats. Let's talk about you!

THE CONTRACT

There is a certain point in this journey that this grows larger than how many points you score or who has bragging rights, especially when you and your parents start investing more commitment of time, sacrifice and money; you both are going to start having goals. Listen to me, the contract or the scholarship is going to become the goal if you keep at this long enough.

Which is why when my son and I arrived at this stage, I saw this as an opportunity to instill the importance of honor, integrity, and character. Also, my son had to realize the potential consequences of signing a contract and not upholding his end of the agreement. He had to understand how it could potentially impact his future. And so will you.

I believe these lessons are better learned with your parents, than with a basketball team or coach who doesn't have the same emotional attachment or responsibility for you as your parents do.

Hence, I wanted to be the first person that my son signed a contract with. So, at the point that I knew that the best fit for him was joining a travel league, I sat down and had a talk with him.

I went over my expectations with him and what he could expect from me. We drafted a contract with each other that was simple and straightforward, outlining our promises to one another.

He promised to keep his grades high; turn in all his homework assignments on time; and finally, he promised that every time he stepped on the court, whether for a practice or a game, that he would give it everything he had.

If he did all those things, I promised, I would support him no matter where this journey took him, down to my last dollar. I am extremely grateful to say that he has been a man of his word, keeping the promises that he made to me that day.

Some of you might be wondering would I potentially stop my son's advancement to the next level because of his academics? What would I have done if his grades dropped, while he was excelling on the basketball court? Would I have pulled the plug on him playing the game that he loved?

My answer is without hesitation, "Yes!"

As a youth athlete, you probably think that to do that to my son would be harsh and uncalled for. But guess what, it is only because my son knew that I would pull the plug, that he held up to his end of the agreement. He did everything that he needed to do to make sure that he upheld his end of the contract.

For some of you, you need to go to your parents and make a contract. You need to put yourself under the obligations to keep your grades up and turn in your homework on time.

Let me stop right here and say this. If you need help in subjects that are harder for you than others, that is NOTHING to be ashamed of. What you should be ashamed of is not asking for academic help when you need it. There are tutors and others who might be right in your inner circle who do well in a subject that you are struggling to understand. Make the effort to be as successful academically as you are athletically. The goal is to be smart and skilled.

I don't want my son limited to one opportunity, nor do I want you to experience limitations. I want him to have the option to choose his path and not have to settle for what's left over if sports don't materialize the way he had hoped. Please hear when I say that I have the very same feelings about who you are and what you are capable of accomplishing.

In the end, there are those who don't agree with me, but I believe as a parent in the journey with a young athlete, academics must be a prerequisite for athletic participation.

My motto has always been this, "Hard work in the classroom and on the field." I believe that you will stand out from the rest and have greater success when you and your parents set boundaries and expectations.

CHARACTER

Student athletics is extremely competitive and can be a slippery slope when it comes to being character driven.

The contract with my son was an exercise of his character as much as it was about anything else.

Colleges are looking for athletes with character now more than ever. Listen to me when I tell you that all the recent rash of incidents on college campuses and the less than honorable character decisions that some professional athletes have made in the past, have oftentimes cost universities and sports franchises more than the athlete was worth in scholarships and ticket sales.

Part of the recruitment process is about your character. Who you are off the court is just as important as what you do on the court. I have personally witnessed youth athletes, both male and female, get passed over for recruitment because of character issues off the court even when they had stellar play on it.

I bring this up in the "Pre-Season" because this is something that you must keep before every decision that you make from the very beginning.

Character is one of those keys that doesn't seem like much until you can't open the door to opportunity without it. The impact of character from the perspective of a college or university starts before the school starts scouting players.

That's what character means to the college and universities that will be recruiting you at the next level. I can't stress this point enough. Character is a crucial aspect of next level success.

ONE SHOT

For the most part, it becomes evident rather early on that you have the talent and desire to play sports. From the time you start, until your Letter of Intent, to the college you choose; you and your parents are only going to have one shot to get this right.

I know it doesn't seem fair, but many times, life isn't fair. With this, there is no room for error. You have ten other student athletes that are just as good as you are waiting on you to make a mistake, so they can take your place.

One of the biggest missteps that I have seen is carelessness on social media. Whether they know if or not, I promise you that many kids have lost their shot because they didn't understand this...everything that you and your family post, and the friends and family that you both are connected to post are being reviewed.

Don't allow the silliness of something as simple as social media to steal the shot that you are working so hard to get. Always remind yourself often to get and keep a clean image. Stay away from controversy and stay focused on the things that are most important.

It's all about the goal ahead for you, and not the many distractions that threaten to derail your progress or stop the options that are on the road ahead of you.

You've made too many sacrifices to allow self-inflicted wounds and poor decisions to have the last say. Like I said, "one shot." Make sure to guard it wisely.

EXPOSURE

Keep this is mind. There are different ways to get noticed. Some good and others not so much. This is why it is important for you to read this book. Because we are going to discuss some of the most effective ways to showcase your skills to increase your chances of getting noticed on the court.

Let's take a closer look.

The following is just my opinion and what I believed was helpful in my son's journey. This may not apply to each individual athlete in their journey.

AAU: Just because you have played on an AAU (Amateur Athletic Union) team doesn't mean that you are getting the exposure necessary to get the proper looks that you need. There are a lot of AAU teams that play travel sports. However, to get noticed you'll need to choose an organization that can place you in the best position to be seen.

You need to understand where college coaches go to recruit kids. Typically, they are going to gravitate towards the organizations that play the toughest competition.

Although there are other areas of AAU play that you can receive exposure, in my experience these four circuits are the most popular.

- The EYBL (Elite Youth Basketball League)
- Adidas Gauntlet
- Under Armour
- NY2LA (New York To Los Angeles)

These circuits attract hundreds of college coaches. Knowing this try to get your parents to place you on a team that's affiliated with one of the above circuits. This will increase their chances of being seen by coaches who are looking for recruits.

High School: In addition to AAU, playing on the high school basketball team can be a good place to gain exposure as well. It's important to know that there are two things that are significant as it relates to getting noticed at the high school level.

- The athlete must be good enough to attract college coaches to come and watch them at the high school level.
- He or she is playing with someone who's good enough to attract college coaches.

Every year there's a period during the high school season where college coaches can come to a high school and watch the students play. This is called "The Open Period." It's during this time where kids get an opportunity to showcase their skills in front of colleges who are looking to add talent to their rosters.

I remember during an "Open Period" when several coaches came to watch my son play. I recall a coach telling me that they also liked several other kids on the team who they originally had not come to see.

It was exciting to think that my son's teammates were getting attention from college coaches that they might not have even expected.

The goal is getting in front of coaches. It doesn't matter who the coach came to see. What matters is that you are there, doing your best every game, every touch, every play.

Let me stop here and interject an important note about high school.

Where my son went to high school was also part of the pre-season stage of his journey. It was important to have him in a school that had a solid academic foundation. We also looked for a high school that he could continue to develop his athletic ability.

His high school played a tremendous role in keeping him focused; educationally and athletically. My family is forever grateful for the years of support that his high school afforded him during his time there.

Keep this in mind when it comes to selecting the high school that you attend if given a choice. Even if it means going out of the district or area that you currently reside to increase your chances for academic and athletic excellence. I believe it is something to consider.

It's important to know how these things work at the high school level so you and your parents have something to work towards. When those college coaches show up, you will be ready. Again, the point here is to just get yourself anywhere where the lights are shining, and you can get noticed.

Recruiting Services: There are a lot of people out there who will tell you that they can do this, or they can do that. In my opinion the most solid way for you to get a scholarship is going to come from hard work and dedication. If it's meant to be, it is going to be the hard work that will eventually put you in a position to develop the relationships with college coaches who may eventually offer you a scholarship.

In my experience if it sounds too good to be true, it probably is. Especially, if the recruiting service is not focused on you maintaining your grades, integrity, and putting in hard work all the way. I was always told growing up that when you have the goods, you don't have to say a word. There will be a path beaten to your doorstep. In other words, put in the work and don't stop because the cream will always rise to the top.

Camps: During the summer there will be a lot of camps being held, some camps are by invitation only and others require a fee to attend. There are also colleges who hold camps to observe talent for potential scholarship opportunities. These camps more than likely will be by invitation only.

What I like about camps is they can be a good source of exposure. However, knowing which camps are worth investing you and your parent's time and effort is important. You must do your research when deciding where to go. In my opinion, it's ok to pay for a camp if the camp is being run by the coaching staff of an actual team. At least you want to be in front of decision makers, and at that point it'll be up to you to showcase your talents to the level of being noticed.

If you're being invited to a camp, more than likely, this means that you have already turned some heads and is being considered as someone who can potentially fit what their program is looking for. If a college specifically invites you to one of their camps, it's a good idea to go. They no doubt have already heard about you and want to take a further look at your skills up close.

My son, Lorne Jr., was invited to multiple camps but the one that stood out to me was from the University of

Wisconsin. When the camp started, I noticed that the head coach and all the assistant coaches were running every aspect of the camp. They were taking notes and paying close attention to each player. It was obvious that they were on a mission to find the best talent. This is what you should be looking for in a camp. My son was in front of the people who could make the decision necessary to determine if an offer would be made. That's all you can ask for as an athlete. The chance to demonstrate your skills in front of the right people.

CAPTURE THE QUEST

Write your definition of 'character'.

_____
_____
_____

Are there any areas where your character can be Improved? How?

_____
_____
_____

What would a Letter of Intent mean to you?

_____
_____
_____

What is one way that you can increase your exposure so that you can get noticed more by coaches and recruiters?

_____
_____
_____

SECTION TWO
REGULAR SEASON RECRUITMENT

Let me start this section by saying how proud I am of you. This is the time to celebrate how far you've come, as much as it is about looking at the work that lies ahead of you in your future. I want you to settle your nerves and gather yourself. Yes, there is a lot going on, but I want you to know out the gate, right now, that you are not in this alone.

One of the benefits of going through this process is all the wonderful people that you are going to meet along the way. You know better than anyone how competitive this sport is, but there are people throughout this journey pulling for you to be successful at every stage. Always remember to appreciate that and never take it for granted.

CAPTURE THE QUEST

Write down at least three people who have helped you reach the recruiting stage of your career.

What are you expecting to get from the recruiting process other than a scholarship? Take a moment to think about this because it will be important later.

THE PURPOSE OF PARTNERSHIP

I was always taught that the best thing you can do when entering into anything is to get a good understanding and gather all the information that you can about what you are about to get involved in.

Not only have I come to understand the great wisdom in this advice, but it has helped me look at everything I do with a desire to know as much as I can about any given situation. Believe me, this one piece of advice has saved me from a whole lot of trouble along the way many times. You are smart enough to understand me when I say that recruiting becomes the start of a partnership that has two sides of the same coin. One side of the coin is the college or university with shiny trinkets and an abundance of opportunities sitting there for you to take.

RECRUITING IS A PARTNERSHIP. And at this stage, I want you to know that you are going to need someone who can help advise you down the recruitment path.

Ideally, it will be your parents, but you will need someone who can look out for your best interest while you are out on the court giving your best performance.

The school is driving the recruiting process and it is very easy to get swept up in the excitement of it all. But I want you to grab your emotions and stay focused on the business of putting in your best effort game after game. The life blood of any school's athletic program is recruiting students. Everyone wants to win and the only way that happens is if the college program gets the best talent they can. Take that knowledge just a bit further by unpacking exactly what that means.

It means that you have value. What it doesn't mean is that you are the only one that has value. Don't walk around with a chip on your shoulder going into this process because there are other athletes that have value too. Stay focused and remain humble.

Think of it this way. You are partnering with the school that you choose when it comes time to sign a Letter of Intent if it gets to that point. Partnership is about you bringing something and the other person bringing something; that's what recruiting is really about. You and your college or university creating a four-year partnership that makes you both happy in the long run.

CAPTURE THE QUEST

Take a moment and think about what you bring to the partnership with a school. List them below.

_____
_____
_____
_____
_____
_____

Now think about some things that the school brings to the partnership. List those below.

_____
_____
_____
_____
_____
_____

Look at both lists. Can you see that you are helping each other to have a positive outcome before, during, and after you complete the partnership?

Please keep this at the forefront of your mind because it is going to guide your attitude during recruitment and as we go further into the process, you are going to find out that a bad attitude can make or break a successful recruitment journey in an instant.

CONSULT YOUR GUARDIAN

One day I noticed a call coming into my phone from a number that I didn't recognize. When I picked up the call there was a man on the other end who said that he as someone who worked for a sports agent.

His words to me were, "We've been watching your son for a while now and have identified him as a pro ball player. We've helped other pros in the past get shoe contracts with the NBA and we'd like to meet with you at our office."

Now keep in mind, my son was only a seventeen-year-old junior in high school at the time. I immediately told him that I'm not interested in anything like that, because my son needs to focus on his grades and choosing a school for college and so do you.

I shared that story to explain how soon you must be focused on taking everything to your parent or guardian when these things start happening. Because lots of decisions that need to be made will need to happen when your parents or guardian decide on the best course of action to take, which will undoubtedly be focused around what's best for you at the time. And there are those who will try to get in the way of that for their own benefit.

As a parent, I understood that they were not calling me for my son's benefit. It wasn't about my son at all, it was about them. Which is why God gave you a guardian in the first place; to watch over and protect you from people and things that come to stop you from being all that you were meant to be.

If I had let my guard down and met with them and let them pay for dinner or I took a gift from them to give my son on their behalf, I would have violated NCAA rules which could have destroyed his scholarship opportunities later on. (We will talk about the NCAA recruiting rules later).

Everybody is not your friend, and these people (who you don't know) are not in your corner. It's up to us as parents to educate ourselves and you about what to do and what not to do during the recruiting process. Sharks lurk in deep water with promises of gifts, money, fame, etc. Now that you are easily accessible through social media that's where the people who want to get close to you will go to approach you. They know that the parents aren't around, and they'll move in and try to latch themselves on to you in a stealth, underhanded type of way.

I recall having to call one coach, in particular, that contacted my son through Twitter when he was a freshman (fourteen years old) in high school asking him a ton of questions that should have been directed to me as his parent. I politely asked him not to reach out to my son again, but he was welcome to call me if he had any other questions regarding my son.

Listen, you can't let your guard down, not even for a second. Always have your guardian in the room with you even though you might be doing the talking. In other words, don't allow your training or regular season process to get too far away from your parents. You should always keep your guardian close and on the pulse of what's going on during your athletic journey.

Keep your guard up and your feet steady.

You must think about these things at the beginning of the recruitment process; not at the point when things start heating up and when the excitement is strong. I encourage you to remember that a partnership is a two-way street—a win-win for both parties involved. Don't step away from the protection your parents provide for you.

One mistake could stop your chances of reaching your goal or seeing your dream become a reality. Always Consult Your Parents.

CAPTURE THE QUEST

Do you have a parent or guardian that you can turn to?

_____
_____
_____

If not, do you have a coach or some other adult that you trust to guide you during this process? _____
If so, who? _____

_____
_____
_____

What would you do?

If a man approached you on SnapChat saying that he is a coach from a university and have been following your career. He knows all your stats, the school you attend, and even names some of your teammates.

He wants to call you offline to discuss you coming to their school in the future.

What would you do in this situation?

_____

_____

_____

_____

_____

_____

I can't say this enough. You have a guardian for a reason. Respect the process and stay under the covering of protection that they provide.

KEEP YOUR EYE ON THE PRIZE

There are many moving components to the recruiting process, but there is one thing that must stay at the forefront of your mind and that is the ultimate goal. With age will come many challenges that will place you in a wrong position if not handled correctly and can result in major setbacks that can stop you from fulfilling your dreams. I want you to understand how critical it is to remember the importance of staying on the right track and keeping your eye on the prize.

I was always taught, and have in turn taught my children, that if it doesn't feel right then remove yourself from the situation; and if it doesn't look right then don't partake in it at all. Trust your instincts and don't override what you know to be the right thing to do. I teach my children that there is NO right way to do wrong and to shun the very appearance of evil. It is inevitable that you will come across compromising situations whether with the opposite sex, hanging around the wrong crowd, or anything that could be a distraction to the plan set before you. Remember one wrong decision can set you back tremendously or destroy everything you've worked so hard for. Be smart, stay focused and keep to the plan.

Let me share a story about the farmer and the horse. One day there was a horse, who was grazing in the field. He stumbled and fell into a very large hole in the ground. When the farmer saw what happened, he determined that the hole was too big to get the horse out of so he wrote the horse off as a lost cause. The farmer decided the only thing to do was to bury the horse right where he stood, however, the horse had other plans. The farmer began to shovel dirt on the horse, but the horse made up his mind that he was gonna keep his eye on the prize which was to get out of that hole.

Therefore, every time the farmer would throw dirt on the horse, the horse would shake it off and pack it under his feet. The farmer continued to throw dirt, but the horse stuck to his plan of shaking it off and packing it under his feet. After a while, something remarkable began to happen and the horse's plan began to work. After hours of shaking off the dirt and packing it under his feet, the horse began to rise out of the hole. Then finally with one last shake and one last pack, he was able to jump out of the hole to safety. The situation that was meant for the horse's doom was turned around for his victory because he devised a plan and kept his eye on the prize.

The moral of the story is to not allow anything to knock you off your square. Don't allow anybody to dictate your outcome; when you make your plan, stick with it, follow it through, stay on guard and I promise that just like that horse, your plan will succeed.

CAPTURE THE QUEST

My ask of you today is simple. Write out your dream. I didn't say athletic dream, I said your dream. Whatever it is, write it down in the space below. Then I want you to reread this section again, and ask yourself, what can I do to make my dream a reality?

_____
_____
_____
_____
_____
_____
_____
_____
_____
_____
_____
_____
_____
_____

DON'T WAIT TOO LONG

As a youth athlete who has their eyes set on recruitment, I'm sure that you have a list of your top three schools that you would like to attend. Let's say hypothetically that all three sports programs contact you at once and ask you to decide to accept their offer.

Could you do it?

The reason I pose this question is simple. You and your parents don't have a long time to decide once an offer is extended. Which is why I suggest planning for best and worst case scenarios long before you start down the journey that is recruitment.

However, if you do feel stuck in your decision once an offer has been extended. Here are a couple tips on how to make the best of the situation and still come out on top.

1. Find out how many other athletes were extended offers as well. This is important because if you have a strong interest in attending that school, in my opinion, it will be

in your best interest not to wait to see what else may or may not come through.

There's an old saying, "A bird in the hand is better than two in the bush." I think this applies here.

2. Look at things from the coaches' perspective. After all, they have a job to do and have been charged with building their athletic programs. Although I am sure that you are talented, I must remind you that you are trying to get a spot with other talented athletes in the running.

When you are targeted as someone they want, time is of the essence. The longer you and your parents allow the offer to sit on the table, the more it reduces the chances of you being a part of that program.

I have a lot of friends who have children that went through and are going through their recruiting journey. One situation stands out to me that I believe is worth mentioning to illustrate this point.

A good buddy of mine has a son that did extremely well in his sport while in high school. He excelled and was considered one of the best players in the state as a senior. He had racked up fifteen scholarship offers during his junior and senior years, but when it came time to commit to one of those fifteen schools, only five were left on the table.

Don't let this happen to you.

Universities don't always wait on the athlete and their family to make up their mind, but instead they move on to the next candidate. I've said this before, recruiting is a two-way street and if there's not much coming back from your side of the street, a school can assume that you may not be as interested in their offer. Again, they will move on to someone who they believe they have a better chance of signing.

    3. You must understand that there are more athletes than scholarships and schools do not like it when kids sit on their offers. They can afford to move on so the real question becomes, can you afford to wait? I was once told by an assistant coach of a major program that if families would educate themselves on how the process works it would make things a

lot easier on them, thus putting the athlete in a much better position overall.

As an athlete, educating yourself is a vital component of the successful outcome for your career. I commend you for picking up this book, because it means that you understand that there are things that you don't know.

I am grateful that at this stage that my son received a full athletic scholarship to a Division I school. My son is happy with the school and academic program that he is now a part of.

I don't expect you to know all the ins and outs of the recruiting process. I can't say this enough, rely on your parents and guardians or other adults to be with you in the trenches, helping you navigate through what can be an overwhelming experience at times.

At the end of the day it's not about seeing how many offers you can stack up, the only thing that does is bolster your ego. Until you commit to a school and sign a national *Letter of Intent* to attend that school, an offer is just verbal communication and nothing more.

CAPTURE THE QUEST

I don't want you to miss your opportunity because you aren't ready. Let's start planning now.

Write out the 3-5 schools that you would like to attend.

- _____
- _____
- _____
- _____
- _____

Also, I want you to think about the dream that you have for yourself in the previous section. Do these schools have programs that align with where you see yourself in the future? I would like you to write down the three schools that have degrees or programs that fit into your career goals below.

- _____
- _____
- _____

Why did I have you do that? I wanted you to realize that these are going to be your top tier schools. That means if any of them come calling, you know to grab your pen, and get ready to sign on the dotted line.

UNDERSTANDING DIVISIONS

For some of you, this section will be just a quick overview of what you already know. Afterall, you have probably been dreaming about the school, and which division you

want to play in for a while now. Some athletes that are just starting their sports journey may need this information.

What are Divisions?

The NCAA Intercollegiate sports are categorized into three divisions.

DIVISION I

Division I schools have:

- The largest student bodies
- The largest athletic budgets

- The highest and most athletic scholarships
- The best athletic facilities

DIVISION II

Division II schools have:

- Smaller student bodies
- Smaller athletic departments and budgets
- Full athletic scholarships are rare (more partial scholarships awarded)

DIVISION III

Division III schools have:

- No athletic scholarships offered
- Most students receive need-based aid
- Less focus on the athletic department

Why is it important to know the differences between divisions? You need to know what your options are when it comes to your athletic career; not all athletic departments are created equal.

Now, let's look at the NCAA and the recruitment calendar that is designed to protect you and regulate the whole recruiting process.

Let's talk about the most prominent governing body of intercollegiate sports athletics, the National Collegiate Athletic Association (NCAA). Many of the college sporting events that are televised like March Madness are competitions within the NCAA. The NCAA was established in part to promote a fair recruiting process and limit the disruptive behavior to the student and their families.

As a student athlete one of the reasons it is imperative that you become familiar with who the NCAA is and what their role is in collegiate sports is because not only do they have prominence in Divisional Leagues, but part of their responsibility is to enforce the rules established within its membership of colleges and universities athletic programs. They oversee everything, from financial aid and scholarships to recruiting and eligibility guidelines.

For the purposes of this book, I will be focusing on the Division I guidelines because Division I teams offer the highest scholarship awards and have the most competitive athletic programs. Most students and their parents aspire to be recruited by this division.

However, again I say, parents must be educated. Therefore, as a student athlete, if there is some information that you know that your parent does not, talk to them so that they can be as informed as possible. This is going to help them make the best decisions for your future!

CAPTURE THE QUEST

Let's review.

How many Divisions does the NCAA have? _____

What does NCAA stand for? _____

_____

What is the main purpose of the NCAA? _____

_____

What makes this important for the athlete and their family?

_____
_____
_____

Lastly, of the three top tier schools on your list which Division is each school under?

SCHOOL	DIVISION
• _____	_____
• _____	_____
• _____	_____

WHAT TIME IS IT?

In recruiting there is a time for everything. The NCAA rules and guidelines are based on a recruiting calendar and every action within that process has a window of opportunity attached to it.

If you are serious about taking your sports journey to the next level, you might already have this calendar memorized. I also suggest that you make a calendar with all these recruiting milestones on it.

It's important to note that the recruiting timetable starts in the middle of your junior year. I don't believe it's ever too soon to start educating yourself and preparing for all the activities that may lay ahead of you.

January—March

During this season, I don't want you to get in the way of opportunity, simply by not paying attention to as many variables as you can. Although I mentioned this idea of behavior and character before, I think it bears reviewing again at this stage.

DON'T GET IN THE WAY

When the time comes for the recruiting process to start, it's important to remember that colleges are looking at you! What you say or do can and will affect you. How you carry yourself speaks volumes.

Coaching staff are doing their homework about you to make sure there are not any questionable character issues, or other potential red flags that they need to know about you and your family.

I know you've had struggles, lived through ups and downs; and even injury. You've had to be consoled after heartbreaking losses. You've had countless hours of training; the thousands of shots in practice; and traveled many places playing game after game.

You've put in literal blood, sweat, and tears; and there is absolutely no way that I want you to do anything to get in the way of what you've worked so hard to accomplish. If you think for a second that your character and image as a player doesn't mean anything, then you're sadly mistaken. Just as good as you play on the court, you are going to have to match that image off the court. What you see in terms of bad behavior in the leagues is no longer tolerated. It costs too much money to deal with athletes who have behavior issues off the court. I tell you again that you or your family can make one poor decision that can ruin your chance at a scholarship. This is something that you and your family must discuss as you go through the recruiting process.

Please keep that in mind as you are taking this time to pull things together to start the recruiting journey. Make a list of what you want to get out of the college experience now. I did this exercise with my son at the beginning of recruitment because I wanted him to take advantage of everything that his college experience had to offer beyond athletics.

I can assure you that when recruitment starts to heat up, you will not have the time or the energy to think with the end in mind. Believe me, now is the time to take advantage of this uninterrupted clarity.

CAPTURE THE QUEST

Name one thing that you can do today to work on your image as a student athlete?

_____
_____
_____

Write a list of things that you want to take from your college experience aside from athletics. Give this some real thought, because I want the same for you as I do for my son. Plan to make the most out of your college experience as you can.

_____
_____
_____
_____
_____

March—May

We talked about this earlier, but these are the months that you and your parents should be reaching out to coaches and letting them know that you are interested in their athletic program (if necessary).

Remind yourselves that coaches will not always know that you exist. Don't be discouraged by this, but it does mean that you may have to do some work to put yourself in the best possible position to be seen. You do this by visiting schools on your short list. Scheduling unofficial visits is a great way to make this happen.

You have put in a whole lot to get here. You have been on the grind this whole time. You have to put as much effort in recruiting as you put on the court.

You should not be surprised if you are on some school's radar, which means you may be asked to participate in different camps over the summer that colleges host to take a better look at potential athletes. You must be prepared for that as a family.

It's to your advantage to attend as many camps (that you're invited to) as you can during the recruiting period. This is a great way for you to showcase your skillset in front of the entire coaching staff. Keep in mind that they extended you an invitation for a reason.

April—August

The only thing that you should be thinking about during this time is playing well. Hopefully, you and your family have done the work and made the financial commitment to visit schools and contact athletic departments.

Don't do all that work and then NOT give the coaches what they are looking for, which is a showcase of your skills, sportsmanship, and potential. Remember to play every game in a way that says, "I'm the student that you want playing for your team!" You must have the mindset to figure out what's going to cause yourself to stand out among the rest of the recruits. Have the mindset that the school is giving something, but they are getting something too—a great student with great athletic ability, and even better attitude and character.

August—November

Up to this point, we have been trying to get as much attention and we can for you and going after anyone who showed some interest. However, it's time to start narrowing down the serious prospects. Which schools are really showing an interest in you? Do those schools have an academic program that is going to align with the education goals that we talked about earlier?

Become focused on what the goal is beyond the four years in college and remove athletics out of the equation. Plan for the next ten years, not just the next four. This exercise is made popular by many CEOs of major corporations and government leaders. What is the ten-year plan? This is going to help steer the four-year selection in a big way!

Unfortunately, your parents can't do this for you. They can want to make decisions for you at this stage, but they can't. As hard as it will be for them, you will need to spur this decision from your own heart.

Of course, parents and guardians will be there to assist, guide, and support, but you must take the freedom to review your options and choose the best one for you.

November—March

You have had the time to sit and consider all the options. I won't lie, it's a little nerve-wracking to watch how this journey is going to play out. I mean, you have been playing this sport for years now. This isn't just an extra-curricular activity; this is part of who you are.

Now something that you have worked for, for such a long time, could open the door to education or other pursuits in a huge way. Know that if you are here at this moment, it wasn't by accident. It was by your hard work, dedication, and commitment to the sport that has gotten you this far. Be thankful no matter what the outcomes are moving forward.

I'm proud of what you have accomplished this far, and you should be proud of yourself too.

CAPTURE THE QUEST

Review the calendar and focus on the key takeaways for each period of the recruiting process. Write down the focus for each period on the recruiting calendar.

January—March

March—May

April—August

August—November

November—March

Keep this list handy and review often to stay on track during the season of recruiting.

SECTION THREE
POST SEASON
CYCLE OF SUCCESS
THE PINNACLE OF THE PROCESS

If you've made it this far in the process, things are getting hot! When I say hot, I mean that things are moving forward at a pretty intense pace. What seemed like a far off journey is now moving along with such momentum, it's hard to keep up. One phone call after another, and decision after decision. Don't forget that you are about to be a high school senior if you aren't one already.

At this point, I have attempted to give you some support and establish more confidence in the recruiting process with a point of view I felt would really help you get in touch with the expectations that are going to be out there. Ultimately, I want you to be able to make better decisions as a youth athlete with a sought after skillset. Now, let's review some crucial information that you will not want to forget.

WHEN RECRUITING HEATS UP

There are Do's and Don'ts of recruiting; I want you to familiarize yourself with some of these basics before the clock starts ticking and the pressure is applied. There are a lot of things that parents don't know, but you should. Which goes back to educating your parents whenever possible. This is to protect you and them.

The Do's and Don'ts

Let's start at the beginning...according to NCAA rules, a school can't contact a potential recruit until **June 15th going into their junior year.** By then if an athlete is going to be recruited, they've already been identified by colleges as someone that they will be reaching out to when the time comes.

In my experience with my son, he received his first piece of mail from a university when he was a freshman in high school. I knew then that his scope of work, between AAU and his high school team had put him on the radar. Receiving letters from schools is a common part of the process; it's a good way to gauge who may be interested in you.

Let's look at this in phases so that you'll know who's flirting with you; who's asking you out; and who's ready to say I do. When you know what stage the relationship is in, you are better able to identify who to respond to. This will inevitably stop you from wasting your family's time with a wink when someone else is standing there with a ring.

Phase 1. (FLIRTING)

As I stated earlier, receiving letters from schools is a good indicator of which programs may be interested in you. This means that the school knows about you and has identified you as a potential recruit. However, it's important to keep everything in perspective because this is just the beginning of the process. You may receive more letters from one school than from others.

At this stage, keep in mind that most of the interest is based on numbers. The coaches have a file with information on potential recruits like, height/weight, scoring, rankings, etc. If you fit what they are looking for on paper, you might be contacted for camp invites or recruiting questionnaires. Some larger athletic programs have an initial recruiting list with thousands of potential recruits. Don't get too excited in this phase. It's just a wink.

Phase 2. (ASKING YOU OUT)

On June 15th, going into your junior year, things will begin to heat up more. Colleges and universities begin to call and text students that they are interested in. You will be able to determine the level of interest based on how many schools are calling, texting, and sending letters to make initial contact with you.

In my experience with my son Lorne Jr., I noticed that he was getting a lot of calls from assistant coaches. I didn't understand until later that one of the primary job responsibilities of an assistant coach is to recruit talent. He or she is assigned to do this so that the head coach can evaluate the potential recruit and ultimately make the determination whether to offer a scholarship or not.

In this phase you'll notice that the assistant coach who is pursuing you may try to get you to the campus on an unofficial visit. According to NCAA rules, you're allowed to take as many unofficial visits as you want. Keep in mind that an unofficial visit is when your parents are responsible for all of your travel expenses (i.e. plane tickets, hotel rooms, spending money etc.) to get to and from their campus. If a school is asking you to come on unofficial visits this is a good indication that you're on their recruiting board, and your name has been coming up in recruiting meetings at that school.

Phase 3. (READY TO SAY I DO)

As Lorne Jr's. recruiting continued to heat up, I noticed that the head coaches began getting involved. They started texting and calling him directly and regularly. In the beginning, the assistant coaches were making all the contact with my son; coming to his school during open gym period; and attending his games, etc. Then I noticed a shift in who was contacting him. The head coaches were coming out to see him play themselves to make their own in-person evaluations of his potential and skill level.

I can vividly recall one day Lorne Jr.'s high school coach called me and said, "I just hung up the phone with the head coach of a major program. He was asking me a ton of questions about your son. He wanted to know about you, his mom, his brother, and his sister. He asked me what type of kid Lorne was, and he wanted his school transcripts."

I said, "WOW!" The next day the head coach called back, and they wanted to come to the school on the following Sunday to see Lorne Jr. play. Because it was a Sunday, Lorne's coach had to arrange a special open gym workout. Just as the workout began, three people walked in -- the head coach, the assistant coach, and the pilot of the private jet they took to fly in to see my son play.

The open gym lasted for two hours. After it was over, they left and flew back home. I didn't know it until later, but it turned out that my son was the only order of business for them that day.

The following day, the head coach texted my son and invited him on an official visit to their campus. **An official visit** is when the school is very interested in you and a scholarship offer is very likely. The school pays for everything, including the plane tickets, hotel, food, etc. Although a kid can receive a scholarship offer on an unofficial visit, the chances of an offer are much higher on an official visit.

In November of his junior year, they flew me and my son to their campus on an official visit. They treated us first class all the way. They picked us up from the airport and immediately took us to their facility where the school's Athletic Director was waiting. He met with us privately to talk about the school and everything it had to offer. After the team practice ended, the head coach took us to his office for a presentation about the program, and what a degree from their university would mean for my son for the rest of his life.

Before he started, he offered my son a full athletic scholarship to attend the university and to play basketball for him and his team. I was blown away by the professionalism and the level of detail in which they approached the recruiting process. It made me realize just how serious recruitment is to the colleges and universities involved.

I'm not saying that every athlete is going to have the same experience that my son had. I'm also not saying that every visit by a college coach will end up in an offer, or that if you receive a letter of interest that it will turn into a signed national *Letter of Intent*.

By no means am I saying that my son was the only choice for the school that he ultimately received his scholarship offer from. I'm humbly saying that as a parent, my child's journey through the recruitment process has shaped me more than I could have ever imagined. Which is why I want you to allow your parents to take this journey with you.

Your parents want you to be successful at whatever you decide to do. Yes, I'm proud and happy for the scholarship offer, but do you know what really makes the recruitment process worthwhile? It's the fact that my son has been given a financial advantage for his life, and the life of his own family years from now. Whether he decides to continue in sports, or take another path, my child is happy to be attending the University of Wisconsin-Madison.

He thinks the pain, the challenges, the shaping, and the breaking was worth it. There is no smooth side to the top of the mountain.

Most athletes will read this and think that this is the end, but they would be wrong. The signed Letter of Intent is just the beginning.

The moment the ink dries is the moment that another season begins; and with it comes a whole new set of challenges, choices, and opportunities that one would never realize could be part of the package. After all, wasn't the scholarship offer to play collegiate sports the goal all along? How could there be more when we reached the goal and finished the journey?

Life is a season of cycles. There will always be another goal, another season, and another cycle that will test your character, perseverance, skill set, and heart for not only this game, but for life in general.

All I can tell you is that the journey never truly ends and there is always something to learn for the rest of your life.

Sports in and of itself is merely a time and place where you will make memories, and touch milestones. Nothing is going to be the same for you after going through the recruitment process whether you continue with sports or not.

My only hope is that reading this book will encourage you to go after your dreams no matter what they are. While giving you a solid understanding that life has challenges along the way, but you must continue to pursue your dreams no matter what comes your way. I believe in you, but I also want you to always believe in yourself. That is what is going to truly make the difference throughout the journey that lies ahead of you.

Until next time, I'll see you in the off-season.

CAPTURE THE QUEST

Answer the following:

What are the three phases of recruitment?

- _____
- _____
- _____

In what phase was Lorne, Jr. in when we were invited to the campus to meet with the head coach?

_____

Who was the person that met with us when we first reached the campus?

_____

Was Lorne's meet with the school considered official or unofficial? _____

What made the difference?

_____
_____
_____

OUR FAMILY
Bowman
TAKING OUR SHOT

ABOUT THE AUTHOR
Lorne Bowman, Sr.

Lorne Bowman, Sr. was born and raised in Detroit, MI; the youngest of 12 children. He resides in Pontiac, MI with his two sons and daughter. Lorne is a poet, songwriter and singer, author, entrepreneur, and a single father. Lorne recognized the extraordinary talent his oldest son had on the basketball court when his son was just four years old. This inspired him to become a basketball trainer so that he could cultivate his son's talents and to be an integral part in his basketball career.

Lorne has devoted his life to raising his children and instilling in them the discipline needed to always strive to reach their full potential. Although challenging at times, Lorne's drive, determination, and commitment over the years were rewarded when, through hard work and dedication his son, Lorne, Jr., earned a full four-year basketball scholarship to the University of Wisconsin.

In hopes of helping other parents and their children realize their dreams, Lorne desires to share the successes he has achieved and setbacks he's endured in helping his son excel in basketball. Through his company, Shots Up LLC, Lorne is dedicated to teaching children the importance of creating and maintaining a clean image, as well as expounding on what's necessary for a child to get off to a good start as they pursue their athletic dreams. In addition, Lorne wants to show every parent how vital it is to educate themselves on the ins and outs of the recruiting process.

Made in the USA
Monee, IL
08 March 2021